The Gateless Gate

The Gateless Gate

All 48 Koans,
with Commentary by Ekai,
called Mumon

WAKING LION PRESS

Cover: The calligraphy in the background is an image of the title page from Mumon's manuscript, *The Gateless Barrier*, or *The Gateless Gate*. (*Mumon* means "Nothing gate" or "No barrier," and the Japanese title of the book is *Mumonkan*, meaning something like "Gateway with no barrier" or "Entrance with no checkpoint.") On the right is an "enso," a circle of enlightenment. The *Shinjinmei*, written in the sixth century, refers to the way of Zen as "a circle like vast space, lacking nothing, and having nothing in excess." One of the earliest references to a written enso occurs in the *Keitokudento-roku*, composed in the eighth century: "A monk asked Master Isan for an ink drawing expressing enlightenment. Isan refused, saying, 'It is right in front of your face. Why should I express it in brush and ink?' The monk then asked Master Kyozan for a drawing. Kyozan made a circle, saying, 'Thinking about this and understanding it is second best; not thinking about it and understanding it is third best.' (He did not specify what is first best.) From then on, the enso became a central theme in Zen art. It can represent the cosmos, the moon, enlightenment, emptiness, change, or the importance of learning the meaning of Zen for oneself rather than filling one's head with the theories of others.

The views expressed in this book are the responsibility of the author and do not necessarily represent the position of The Editorium. The reader alone is responsible for the use of any ideas or information provided by this book.

ISBN 9781434119155

Published by Waking Lion Press, an imprint of The Editorium

Additions to original text © 2006 by The Editorium. All rights reserved. Printed in the United States of America.

Waking Lion Press™, the Waking Lion Press logo, and The Editorium™ are trademarks of The Editorium, LLC

The Editorium, LLC
West Valley City, UT 84128-3917
wakinglionpress.com
wakinglion@editorium.com

Contents

Preface by Mumon		ix
1	Joshu's Dog	1
2	Hyakujo's Fox	3
3	Gutei's Finger	5
4	A Beardless Foreigner	7
5	Kyogen Mounts the Tree	9
6	Buddha Twirls a Flower	11
7	Joshu Washes the Bowl	13
8	Keichu's Wheel	15
9	A Buddha Before History	17
10	Seizei Alone and Poor	19
11	Joshu Examines a Monk in Meditation	21
12	Zuigan Calls His Own Master	23
13	Tokusan Holds His Bowl	25
14	Nansen Cuts the Cat in Two	27
15	Tozan's Three Blows	29
16	Bells and Robes	31
17	The Three Calls of the Emperor's Teacher	33
18	Tozan's Three Pounds	35

19 Everyday Life Is the Path	37
20 The Enlightened Man	39
21 Dried Dung	41
22 Kashapa's Preaching Sign	43
23 Eno's Good and Not-Good	45
24 Without Words, Without Silence	47
25 Preaching from the Third Seat	49
26 Two Monks Roll Up the Screen	51
27 It Is Not Mind, It Is Not Buddha, It Is Not Things	53
28 Blow Out the Candle	55
29 Not the Wind, Not the Flag	57
30 This Mind Is Buddha	59
31 Joshu Investigates	61
32 A Philosopher Asks Buddha	63
33 Neither Mind Nor Buddha	65
34 Nansen's No Way	67
35 Two Souls	69
36 Goso's No Words, No Silence	71
37 Joshu's Oak Tree in the Garden	73
38 Goso's Buffalo	75
39 Ummon and the Word Trap	77
40 Kicking the Water Jar	79
41 Bodhidharma's Peace of Mind	81
42 A Woman Comes Out of Meditation	83
43 Shuzan's Bamboo Spatula	85
44 Basho's Staff	87

45 Who Is He?	89
46 Proceed Beyond the Top of the 100-Foot-High Pole	91
47 Tosotsu's Three Barriers	93
48 The One Road of Kempo	95
Epilogue by Mumon	97

Preface by Mumon

Our teaching makes our mind the principle, and the gateless gate its very gate. Since it is gateless, how can one pass through it?

Are you not aware of the insight that purports, "Those who have entered the gate are no family treasures; what is gained as a result of cause and effect has beginning and end, and thus will become nothing"? Such remarks are like raising up waves in the windless ocean, or gouging a wound into healthy skin. Those who cling to words are fools who believe that they can catch the moon with a stick or scratch their itchy foot through a leather shoe. How can they "see" reality as it actually is?

In the summer of the first year of Shjoting [1228], Ekai [Mumon] was lecturing on koan of the ancient masters to the monks at the monastery of Luinghsiang temple in East China. He intended to use the koan as bricks for battering the gate in order to inspire the pursuer of Zen according to his ability. His notes were unwittingly collected. There is no order as to the beginning or the end. In total there are 48 cases, now called "The Gateless Gate."

If anyone, like eight-armed Nata who bravely goes straight forward, ventures into Zen practice, no delusion will disturb him. The Indian and Chinese patriarchs will beg for their lives in his commanding presence. If, however, he hesitates even a moment, he is just a person that watches from a narrow window for a speedy horseman to pass by and misses everything in a wink.

The Great Way has no gate,
A thousand roads enter it.
When one passes through this gateless gate,
He freely walks between heaven and earth.

Case 1

Joshu's Dog

A monk asked Joshu, a Chinese Zen master: "Has a dog Buddha-nature or not?"

Joshu answered: "Mu." ["No-thing" or "No."]

Mumon's Comment

To realize Zen, one has to pass through the barrier of the patriarchs. Enlightenment always comes after the road of thinking is blocked. If you do not pass the barrier of the patriarchs, or if your thinking road is not blocked, whatever you think, whatever you do, is like a tangling ghost. You may ask: What is a barrier of a patriarch? This one word, *Mu,* is it.

This is the barrier of Zen. If you pass through it, you will see Joshu face to face. Then you can work hand in hand with the whole line of patriarchs. Is this not a pleasant thing to do?

If you want to pass this barrier, you must work through every bone in your body, through every pore in your skin, filled with this question: What is Mu? and carry it day and night. Do not believe it is the common negative symbol meaning nothing. It is not nothingness, the opposite of existence. If you really want to pass this barrier, you should feel as if you are drinking a hot iron ball that you can neither swallow nor spit out.

Then your previous lesser knowledge disappears. As a fruit ripening in season, your subjectivity and objectivity naturally become one. It is like a dumb man who has had a dream; he knows about it but cannot tell it.

When he enters this condition his ego-shell is crushed, and he can shake the heaven and move the earth. He is like a great warrior with a sharp sword. If a Buddha stands in his way, he will cut him down; if a patriarch offers him any obstacle, he will kill him; and he will be free in this way of birth and death. He can enter any world as if it were his own playground. I will tell you how to do this with this koan:

Just concentrate your whole energy into this Mu, and do not allow any discontinuation. When you enter this Mu and there is no discontinuation, your attainment will be as a candle burning and illuminating the whole universe.

    Has a dog Buddha-nature?
    This is the most serious question of all.
    If you say yes or no,
    You lose your own Buddha-nature.

Case 2

Hyakujo's Fox

Once when Hyakujo delivered some Zen lectures, an old man attended them, unseen by the monks. At the end of each talk when the monks left, so did he. But one day he remained after they had gone, and Hyakujo asked him: "Who are you?"

The old man replied: "I am not a human being, but I was a human being when the Kashapa Buddha preached in this world. I was a Zen master and lived on this mountain. At that time, one of my students asked me whether the enlightened man is subject to the law of causation. I answered him: 'The enlightened man is not subject to the law of causation.' For this answer evidencing a clinging to absoluteness, I became a fox for five hundred rebirths, and I am still a fox. Will you save me from this condition with your Zen words and let me get out of a fox's body? Now may I ask you: Is the enlightened man subject to the law of causation?"

Hyakujo said: "The enlightened man is one with the law of causation."

At the words of Hyakujo, the old man was enlightened. "I am emancipated," he said, paying homage with a deep bow. "I am no more a fox, but I have to leave my body in my dwelling place behind this mountain. Please perform my funeral as a monk." Then he disappeared.

The next day Hyakujo gave an order through the chief monk to prepare to attend the funeral of a monk. "No one was sick in the infirmary," wondered the monks. "What does our teacher mean?"

After dinner Hyakujo led the monks out and around the mountain. In a cave, with his staff he poked out the corpse of an old fox and then performed the ceremony of cremation.

That evening Hyakujo gave a talk to the monks and told this story about the law of causation.

Obaku, upon hearing this story, asked Hyakujo: "I understand that a long time ago because a certain person gave a wrong Zen answer he became a fox for five hundred rebirths. Now I want to ask: If some modern master is asked many questions, and he always gives the right answer, what will become of him?"

Hyakujo said: "You come here near me and I will tell you."

Obaku went near Hyakujo and slapped the teacher's face with this hand, for he knew this was the answer his teacher intended to give him.

Hyakujo clapped his hands and laughed at the discernment. "I thought a Persian had a red beard," he said, "and now I know a Persian who has a red beard."

Mumon's Comment

"The enlightened man is not subject." How can this answer make the monk a fox?

"The enlightened man is at one with the law of causation." How can this answer make the fox emancipated?

To understand clearly, one has to have just one eye.

Controlled or not controlled?
The same dice shows two faces.
Not controlled or controlled,
Both are a grievous error.

Case 3

Gutei's Finger

Gutei raised his finger whenever he was asked a question about Zen. A boy attendant began to imitate him in this way. When anyone asked the boy what his master had preached about, the boy would raise his finger.

Gutei heard about the boy's mischief. He seized him and cut off his finger. The boy cried and ran away. Gutei called and stopped him. When the boy turned his head to Gutei, Gutei raised up his own finger. In that instant the boy was enlightened.

When Gutei was about to pass from this world, he gathered his monks around him. He said: "I attained my finger-Zen from my teacher Tenryu, and in my whole life I could not exhaust it." Then he passed away.

Mumon's Comment

Enlightenment, which Gutei and the boy attained, has nothing to do with a finger. If anyone clings to a finger, Tenyru will be so disappointed that he will annihilate Gutei, the boy, and the clinger all together.

> Gutei cheapens the teaching of Tenyru,
> Emancipating the boy with a knife.
> Compared to the Chinese god who pushed aside a
>   mountain with one hand,

Old Gutei is a poor imitator.

Case 4

A Beardless Foreigner

Wakun complained when he saw a picture of the bearded Bodhidharma: "Why hasn't that fellow a beard?"

Mumon's Comment

If you want to study Zen, you must do it with your heart. When you attain realization, it must be true realization. You yourself must have the face of the great Bodhidharma to see him. Just one such glimpse will be enough. But if you say you met him, you never saw him at all.

> One should not discuss a dream
> In front of a simpleton.
> Why has Bodhidharma no beard?
> What an absurd question!

Case 5

Kyogen Mounts the Tree

Kyogen said: "Zen is like a man hanging in a tree by his teeth over a precipice. His hands grasp no branch, his feet rest on no limb, and under the tree another person asks him: 'Why did Bodhidharma come to China from India?' If the man in the tree does not answer, he fails [to demonstrate his understanding of Zen]; and if he does answer, he falls and loses his life. Now what shall he do?"

Mumon's Comment

In such a predicament, the most talented eloquence is no use. If you have memorized all the sutras, you cannot use them. When you can give the right answer, even though your past road was one of death, you open up a new road of life. But if you cannot answer, you should wait for ages hence and ask Maitreya, the future Buddha.

Kyogen is truly a fool,
Spreading that ego-killing poison
That closes his pupils' mouths
And lets their tears stream from their dead eyes.

Case 6

Buddha Twirls a Flower

When Buddha was in Grdhrakuta mountain, he turned a flower in his fingers and held it before his listeners. Everyone was silent. Only Maha-Kashapa smiled at this revelation, although he tried to control the lines of his face.
Buddha said: "I have the eye of the true teaching, the heart of Nirvana, the true aspect of non-form, and the ineffable stride of Dharma. It is not expressed by words but especially transmitted beyond teaching. This teaching I have given to Maha-Kashapa."

Mumon's Comment

Golden-faced Guatama thought he could cheat anyone. He made the good listeners as bad, and sold dog meat under the sign of mutton. And he himself thought it was wonderful. What if all the audience had laughed together? How could he have transmitted the teaching? And again, if Maha-Kashapa had not smiled, how could he have transmitted the teaching? If he says that realization can be transmitted, he is like the city slicker that cheats the country dub, and if he says it cannot be transmitted, why does he approve of Maha-Kashapa?

At the turning of a flower
His diguise was exposed.

No one in heaven or earth can surpass
Maha-Kashapa's wrinkled face.

Case 7

Joshu Washes the Bowl

A monk told Joshu: "I have just entered the monastery. Please teach me." Joshu asked: "Have you eaten your rice porridge?" The monk replied: "I have eaten." Joshu said: "Then you had better wash your bowl." At that moment the monk was enlightened.

Mumon's Comment

Joshu is the man who opens his mouth and shows his heart. I doubt if this monk really saw Joshu's heart. I hope he did not mistake the bell for a pitcher.

> It is too clear, and so it is hard to see.
> A dunce once searched for fire with a lighted lantern.
> Had he known what fire was,
> He could have cooked his rice much sooner.

Case 8

Keichu's Wheel

Getsuan said to his students: "Keichu, the first wheel-maker of China, made two wheels of fifty spokes each. Now, suppose you removed the hub uniting the spokes. What would become of the wheel? And had Keichu done this, could he be called the master wheel-maker?"

Mumon's Comment

If anyone can answer this question instantly, his eyes will be like a comet, and his mind like a flash of lightning.

When the hubless wheel turns,
Master or no master can stop it.
It turns above heaven and below earth,
South, north, east, and west.

Case 9

A Buddha Before History

A monk asked Seijo: "I understand that Daitsu Chisho Buddha, who lived before recorded history, sat in meditation for ten cycles of existence and could not realize the highest truth, and so could not become fully emancipated. Why was this so?"

Seijo replied: "Your question is self-explanatory."

The monk asked: "Since the Buddha was meditating, why could he not fulfill Buddhahood?" Seijo said: "He was not a Buddha."

Mumon's Comment

I will allow his realization, but I will not admit his understanding. When one ignorant attains realization, he is a saint. When a saint begins to understand, he is an ignorant.

It is better to realize mind than body.
When the mind is realized, one need not worry about body.
When mind and body become one,
The man is free. Then he desires no praising.

Case 10

Seizei Alone and Poor

A monk named Seizei asked of Sozan: "Seizei is alone and poor. Will you give him support?"
Sozan asked: "Seizei?"
Seizei responded: "Yes, sir."
Sozan said: "You have Zen, the best wine in China, and already have finished three cups, and still you are saying that they did not even wet your lips."

Mumon's Comment

Seizei overplayed his hand. Why was it so? Because Sozan had eyes and knew with whom he was dealing. Even so, I want to ask: At what point did Seizei drink wine?

The poorest man in China,
The bravest man in China,
He barely sustains himself,
Yet wishes to rival the wealthiest.

Case 11

Joshu Examines a Monk in Meditation

Joshu went to a place were a monk had retired to meditate and asked him: "What is, is what?" The monk raised his fist.

Joshu replied: "Ships cannot remain where the water is too shallow." And he left. A few days later, Joshu went again to visit the monk and asked the same question. The monk answered the same way.

Joshu said: "Well given, well taken, well killed, well saved." And he bowed to the monk.

Mumon's Comment

The raised fist was the same both times. Why is it Joshu did not admit the first and approved the second one? Where is the fault?

Whoever answers this knows that Joshu's tongue has no bone so he can use it freely. Yet perhaps Joshu is wrong. Or, through that monk, he may have discovered his mistake.

If anyone thinks that the one's insight exceeds the other's, he has no eyes.

> The light of the eyes is as a comet,
> And Zen's activity is as lightning.
> The sword that kills the man
> Is the sword that saves the man.

Case 12

Zuigan Calls His Own Master

Zuigan called out to himself every day: "Master."
Then he answered himself: "Yes, sir."
And after that he added: "Wake up!"
Again he answered: "Yes, sir."
He continued: "And after that, do not be deceived by others."
He answered: "Yes, sir; yes, sir."

Mumon's Comment

Old Zuigan sells out and buys himself. He is opening a puppet show. He uses one mask to call "Master" and another that answers the master.

Another mask says "Sober up," and another "Don't be cheated by others." If anyone clings to any of his masks, he is mistaken, yet if he imitates Zuigan, he will make himself fox-like.

Some Zen students do not realize the true man in a mask
Because they recognize ego-soul.
Ego-soul is the seed of birth and death,
And foolish people call it the true man [true self].

Case 13

Tokusan Holds His Bowl

Tokusan went to the dining room from the meditation hall holding his bowl. Seppo was on duty cooking. When he met Tokusan he said: "The dinner drum is not yet beaten. Where are you going with your bowl?"

So Tokusan returned to his room.

Seppo told Ganto about this. Ganto said: "Old Tokusan did not understand the ultimate truth."

Tokusan heard of this remark and asked Ganto to come to him. "I have heard," he said, "you are not approving my Zen." Ganto admitted this indirectly [whispered to Tokusan what he meant]. Tokusan said nothing.

The next day Tokusan delivered an entirely different kind of lecture to the monks. Ganto laughed and clapped his hands, saying: "I see our old man understands the ultimate truth indeed. None in China can surpass him."

Mumon's Comment

Speaking about ultimate truth, both Ganto and Tokusan did not even dream it. After all, they are dummies.

Whoever understands the first truth
Should understand the ultimate truth.
The last and first,

Are they not the same?

Case 14

Nansen Cuts the Cat in Two

Nansen saw the monks of the eastern and western halls fighting over a cat. He seized the cat and told the monks: "If any of you say a good word [a word of Zen], you can save the cat."

No one answered. So Nansen boldly cut the cat in two pieces.

That evening Joshu returned, and Nansen told him about this. Joshu removed his sandals and, placing them on his head, walked out.

Nansen said: "If you had been there, you could have saved the cat."

Mumon's Comment

Why did Joshu put his sandals on his head? If anyone answers this question with one word, he will understand exactly how Nansen enforced the edict. If not, he should watch his own head.

> Had Joshu been there,
> He would have enforced the edict oppositely.
> Joshua snatches the sword,
> And Nansen begs for his life.

Case 15

Tozan's Three Blows

Tozan went to Ummon. Ummon asked him where he had come from.
Tozan said: "From Sato village."
Ummon asked: "In what temple did you remain for the summer?"
Tozan replied: "The temple of Hoji, south of the lake." Wondering how long Tozan would continue with such factual answers, Ummon asked: "When did you leave there?"
Tozan answered: "The twenty-fifth of August."
Ummon said: "I should give you three blows with a stick, but today I forgive you."
The next day Tozan bowed to Ummon and asked: "Yesterday you forgave me three blows. I do not know why you thought me wrong." Ummon, rebuking Tozan's spiritless responses, said: "You are good for nothing. You simply wander from one monastery to another." Before Ummon's words were ended, Tozan was enlightened.

Mumon's Comment

Ummon fed Tozan good Zen food. If Tozan can digest it, Ummon may add another member to his family.
In the evening Tozan swam around in a sea of good and bad, but at dawn Ummon crushed his nut shell. After all, he wasn't so smart.

Now, I want to ask: Did Tozan deserve the three blows? If you say yes, not only Tozan but every one of you deserves them. If you say no, Ummon is speaking a lie. If you answer this question clearly, you can eat the same food as Tozan.

The lioness teaches her cubs roughly;
The cubs jump and she knocks them down.
When Ummon saw Tozan, his first arrow was light;
His second arrow shot deep.

Case 16

Bells and Robes

Ummon asked: "The world is so wide; why do you answer a bell and don ceremonial robes?"

Mumon's Comment

When one studies Zen one need not follow sound or color or form. Even though some have attained insight when hearing a voice or seeing a color or a form, this is a very common way. It is not true Zen. The real Zen student controls sound, color, form, and actualizes the truth in his everyday life.

Sound comes to the ear, the ear goes to the sound. When you blot out sound and sense, what do you understand? While listening with ears one never can understand. To understand intimately one should see sound.

When you understand, you belong to the family;
When you do not understand, you are a stranger.
Those who do not understand belong to the family,
And when they understand they are strangers.

Case 17

The Three Calls of the Emperor's Teacher

Chu, called Kokushi, the teacher of the emperor, called to his attendant: "Oshin."
Oshin answered: "Yes."
Chu repeated, to test his pupil: "Oshin."
Oshin repeated: "Yes."
Chu called: "Oshin."
Oshin answered: "Yes." Chu said: "I ought to apologize to you for all this calling, but really you ought to apologize to me."

Mumon's Comment

When Old Chu called Oshin three times, his tongue was rotting, but when Oshin answered three times his words were brilliant. Chu was getting decrepit and lonesome, and his method of teaching was like holding a cow's head to feed it clover.

Oshin did not trouble to show his Zen either. His satisfied stomach had no desire to feast. When the country is prosperous everyone is indolent; when the home is wealthy the children are spoilt.

Now I want to ask you: Which one should apologize?

When prison stocks are iron and have no place for the head,

The prisoner is doubly in trouble.
When there is no place for Zen in the head of our
 generation,
It is in grievous trouble.
If you try to hold up the gate and door of a falling house,
You also will be in trouble.

Case 18

Tozan's Three Pounds

A monk asked Tozan when he was weighing some flax: "What is Buddha?"
Tozan said: "Three pounds of flax."

Mumon's Comment

Old Tozan's Zen is like a clam. The minute the shell opens, you see the whole inside. However, I want to ask you: Do you see the real Tozan?

Three pounds of flax in front of your nose,
Close enough, and mind is still closer.
Whoever talks about affirmation and negation
Lives in the right and wrong region.

Case 19

Everyday Life Is the Path

Joshu asked Nansen: "What is the path?"
Nansen said: "Everyday life is the path."
Joshu asked: "Can it be studied?"
Nansen said: "If you try to study, you will be far away from it."
Joshu asked: "If I do not study, how can I know it is the path?"
Nansen said: "The path does not belong to the world of perception [knowledge], neither does it belong to the non-perception world. Cognition is a delusion, and noncognition is senseless. [Knowledge is illusion, and non-knowledge is beyond discrimination.] If you want to reach the true path beyond doubt, place yourself in the same freedom as sky. You name it neither good nor not-good."
At these words Joshu was enlightened.

Mumon's Comment

Nansen could meet Joshu's frozen doubts at once when Joshu asked his questions. I doubt that Joshu reached the point that Nansen did. He needed thirty more years of study.

> In spring, hundreds of flowers; in autumn, a harvest moon;
> In the summer, a refreshing breeze; in winter, snow will accompany you.

If useless things do not hang in your mind,
Any season is a good season for you.

Case 20

The Enlightened Man

Shogen asked: "Why does the enlightened man not stand on his feet and explain himself [demonstrate understanding of Zen]?" And he also said: "It is not necessary for speech to come from the tongue."

Mumon's Comment

Shogen spoke plainly enough, but how many will understand? If anyone comprehends, he should come to my place and test out my big stick. Why, look here, to test [know] real gold you must see it through fire.

> If the feet of enlightenment moved, the great ocean would overflow;
> If that head bowed, it would look down upon the heavens.
> Such a body has no place to rest . . .
> Let another [the reader] continue this poem.

Case 21

Dried Dung

A monk asked Ummon: "What is Buddha?"
Ummon answered him: "Dried dung."

Mumon's Comment

It seems to me Ummon is so poor he cannot distinguish the taste of one food from another, or else he is too busy to write readable letters. Well, he tried to hold his school with dried dung. And his teaching was just as useless.

Lightning flashes,
Sparks shower.
In one blink of your eyes
You have missed seeing.

Case 22

Kashapa's Preaching Sign

Ananda asked Kashapa: "Buddha gave you the golden-woven robe of successorship. What else did he give you?"
Kashapa said: "Ananda."
Ananda answered: "Yes, brother."
Said Kashapa: "Now you can take down my preaching sign and put up your own."

Mumon's Comment

If one understands this, he will see the old brotherhood still gathering, but if not, even though he has studied the truth from ages before the Buddhas, he will not attain enlightenment.

> The point of the question is dull, but the answer is intimate.
> How many persons hearing it will open their eyes?
> Elder brother calls and younger brother answers;
> This spring does not belong to the ordinary season.

Case 23

Eno's Good and Not-Good

When he became enlightened, Eno (the sixth patriarch) received from the fifth patriarch the bowl and robe given from the Buddha to his successors, generation after generation. A monk named E-myo, out of envy, pursued the patriarch to take this great treasure away from him. The sixth patriarch placed the bowl and robe on a stone in the road and told E-myo: "These objects just symbolize the faith. There is no use fighting over them. If you desire to take them, take them now."

When E-myo went to move the bowl and robe, they were as heavy as mountains. He could not budge them. Trembling for shame he said: "I came wanting the teaching, not the material treasures. Please teach me."

The sixth patriarch said: "When you do not think good and when you do not think not-good, what is your true self?"

At these words E-myo was illumined. Perspiration broke out all over his body. He cried and bowed, saying: "You have given me the secret words and meanings. Is there yet a deeper part of the teaching?"

The sixth patriarch replied: "What I have told you is no secret at all. When you realize your true self, the secret belongs to you."

E-myo said: "I was under the fifth patriarch for many years but could not realize my true self until now. Through your teaching I find the source. A person drinks water and knows for himself whether it is cold or warm. May I call you my teacher?"

The sixth patriarch replied: "We studied together under the fifth patriarch. Call him your teacher, but just treasure what you have attained."

Mumon's Comment

The sixth patriarch certainly was kind in such an emergency. It was as if he removed the skin and seeds from the fruit and then, opening the pupil's mouth, let him eat.

> You cannot describe it, you cannot picture it,
> You cannot admire it, you cannot sense it.
> It is your true self; it has nowhere to hide.
> When the world is destroyed, it will not be destroyed.

Case 24

Without Words, Without Silence

A monk asked Fuketsu: "Without speaking, without silence, how can you express the truth?"

Fuketsu observed: "I always remember springtime in southern China. The birds sing among innumerable kinds of fragrant flowers."

Mumon's Comment

Fuketsu used to have lightning Zen. Whenever he had the opportunity, he flashed it. But this time he failed to do so and only borrowed from an old Chinese poem. Never mind Fuketsu's Zen. If you want to express the truth, throw out your words, throw out your silence, and tell me about your own Zen.

> Without revealing his own penetration,
> He offered another's words, not his to give.
> Had he chattered on and on,
> Even his listeners would have been embarassed.

Case 25

Preaching from the Third Seat

In a dream Kyozen went to Maitreya's Pure Land. He recognized himself seated in the third seat in the abode of Maitreya. Someone announced: "Today the one who sits in the third seat will preach."

Kyozen arose and, hitting the gavel, said: "The truth of Mahayana teaching is transcendent, above words and thought. Do you understand?" ["The truth of Mahayana is beyond any verbal expression! Listen, listen!"]

Mumon's Comment

I want to ask you monks: Did he preach or did he not?

When he opens his mouth he is lost. When he seals his mouth he is lost. If he does not open it, if he does not seal it, he is 108 thousand miles from the truth.

In the light of day,
Yet in a dream he talks of a dream.
A monster among monsters,
He intended to deceive the whole crowd.

Case 26

Two Monks Roll Up the Screen

Hogen of Seiryo monastery was about to lecture before dinner when he noticed that the bamboo screen lowered for meditation had not been rolled up. He pointed to it. Two monks arose from the audience and rolled it up. Hogen, observing the physical moment, said: "The state of the first monk is good, not that of the other."

Mumon's Comment

I want to ask you: Which of those two monks gained and which lost? If any of you has one eye, he will see through the failure of the teacher's. However, I am not discussing gain and loss.

When the screen is rolled up, the great sky opens,
Yet the sky is not attuned to Zen.
It is best to forget the great sky
And to retire from every wind.

Case 27

It Is Not Mind, It Is Not Buddha, It Is Not Things

A monk asked Nansen: "Is there a teaching no master ever preached before?"
Nansen said: "Yes, there is."
The monk asked: "What is it?"
Nansen replied: "It is not mind, it is not Buddha, it is not things."

Mumon's Comment

Old Nansen gave away his treasure-words. He must have been greatly upset.

Nansen was too kind and lost his treasure.
Truly, words have no power.
Even though the mountain becomes the sea,
Words cannot open another's mind.

Case 28

Blow Out the Candle

Tokusan was studying Zen under Ryutan. One night he came to Ryutan and asked many questions. The teacher said: "The night is getting old. Why don't you retire?"

So Tukusan bowed and opened the screen to go out, observing: "It is very dark outside."

Ryutan offered Tokusan a lighted candle to find his way. Just as Tokusan received it, Ryutan blew it out. At that moment the mind of Tokusan was opened. Ryutan asked: "What have you attained?"

Tokusan said: "From now on, I will not doubt the teacher's words."

The next day Ryutan told the monks at his lecture: "I see one monk among you. His teeth are like the sword tree, his mouth is like the blood bowl. If you hit him hard with a big stick, he will not even so much as look back at you. Someday he will mount the highest peak and carry my teaching there."

On that day, in front of the lecture hall, Tokusan burned to ashes his commentaries on the sutras. He said: "However abstruse the teachings are, in comparison with this enlightenment they are like a single hair to the great sky. However profound the complicated knowledge of the world, compared to this enlightenment it is like one drop of water to the great ocean."

Then he left the monastry.

Mumon's Comment

Before Tokusan passed through the barrier, his mind was eager, his mouth was anxious; with a purpose in his mind, he went south, to refute the doctrine of "A special transmission outside the sutras." So he traveled south. He happened to stop near Ryutan's monastery for refreshments. An old woman who was there asked him: "What are you carrying so heavily?"

Tokusan replied: "This is a commentary I have made on the Diamond Sutra after many years of work."

The old woman said: "I read that sutra which says: 'The past mind cannot be held, the present mind cannot be held, the future mind cannot be held.' You wish some tea and refreshments. Which mind do you propose to use for them?"

Tokusan was as though dumb. Finally he asked the woman: "Do you know of any good teacher around here?"

The old woman referred him to Ryutan, not more than five miles away. So he went to Ryutan in all humility, quite different from when he had started his journey. Ryutan in turn was so kind he forgot his own dignity. It was like pouring muddy water over a drunken man to sober him. After all, it was an unnecessary comedy.

> A hundred hearings cannot surpass one seeing,
> But after you see the teacher, that once glance cannot
>   surpass a hundred hearings.
> His nose was very high
> But he was blind after all.

Case 29

Not the Wind, Not the Flag

Two monks were arguing about a flag. One said: "The flag is moving."
The other said: "The wind is moving."
The sixth patriarch happened to be passing by. He told them: "Not the wind, not the flag; mind is moving."

Mumon's Comment

The sixth patriarch said: "The wind is not moving, the flag is not moving. Mind is moving." What did he mean? If you understand this intimately, you will see the two monks there trying to buy iron and gaining gold. The sixth patriarch could not bear to see those two dull heads, so he made such a bargain.

Wind, flag, mind moves.
The same understanding.
When the mouth opens,
All are wrong.

Case 30

This Mind Is Buddha

Daibai asked Baso: "What is Buddha?"
Baso said: "This mind is Buddha."

Mumon's Comment

If anyone wholly understands this, he is wearing Buddha's clothing, he is eating Buddha's food, he is speaking Buddha's words, he is behaving as Buddha, he is Buddha.

This anecdote, however, has given many pupils the sickness of formality. If one truly understands, he will wash out his mouth for three days after saying the word *Buddha,* and he will close his ears and flee after hearing "This mind is Buddha."

Under blue sky, in bright sunlight,
One need not search around.
Asking what Buddha is
Is like hiding loot in one's pocket and declaring oneself
   innocent.

Case 31

Joshu Investigates

A traveling monk asked an old woman about the road to Taizan, a popular temple supposed to give wisdom to the one who worships there. The old woman said: "Go straight ahead." When the monk proceeded a few steps, she said to herself: "He also is a common church-goer."

Someone told this incident to Joshu, who said: "Wait until I investigate." The next day he went and asked the same question, and the old woman gave the same answer. Joshu remarked: "I have investigated that old woman."

Mumon's Comment

The old woman understood how war is planned, but she did not know how spies sneak in behind her tent. Old Joshu played the spy's work and turned the tables on her, but he was not an able general. Both had their faults. Now I want to ask you: What was the point of Joshu's investigating the old woman?

When the question is common,
The answer is also common.
When the question is sand in a bowl of boiled rice,
The answer is a stick in the soft mud.

Case 32

A Philosopher Asks Buddha

A philosopher asked Buddha: "Without words, without the wordless, will you tell me truth?"

The Buddha kept silence. The philosopher bowed and thanked the Buddha, saying: "With your loving kindness I have cleared away my delusions and entered the true path."

After the philosopher had gone, Ananda asked the Buddha what he had attained.

The Buddha replied, "A good horse runs even at the shadow of the whip."

Mumon's Comment

Ananda was the disciple of the Buddha. Even so, his opinion did not surpass that of outsiders. I want to ask you monks: How much difference is there between disciples and outsiders?

To tread the sharp edge of a sword,
To run on smooth-frozen ice,
One needs no footsteps to follow.
Walk over the cliffs with hands free.

Case 33

Neither Mind Nor Buddha

A monk asked Baso, "What is the Buddha?"
Baso replied, "Not mind, not Buddha."

Mumon's Comment

If anyone understands what Baso said, he has mastered Zen.
If you meet a sword master on the road, give him the sword.
Unless you meet a poet on the road, do not offer a poem.
If you meet a man, tell him the three quarters of the Way, and never tell him the rest.

Case 34

Nansen's No Way

Nansen said, "Mind is not Buddha. Knowledge is not the Way."

Mumon's Comment

Growing old, Nansen forgot to be ashamed. With his stinking mouth open, he spread the scandal of his own house (such as knowledge is not the Way) to others. However, few appreciate their indebtedness to him.

When the sky is clear, the sun appears;
When rain falls, the earth becomes moistened.
How wholeheartedly he explains;
How few have faith in him and his words.

Case 35

Two Souls

Goso asked a monk, "Sei, the Chinese girl, who was separated from her soul—which was the real Sei?"

Mumon's Comment

If you obtain genuine awareness of reality, you will know that the soul passes from one husk to another as travelers lodged in an inn. But if you have not obtained the awareness, you should not run around in confusion when the four elements are suddenly ready to become separated [that is, die] like a crab with its seven arms and eight legs thrown into the boiling water. Never say that I did not warn you.

The moon in the clouds is one and the same,
Valleys and mountains are various.
Fortunes above fortunes,
Is it one, or is it two?

Case 36

Goso's No Words, No Silence

Goso said, "When you meet a Man of the Way on the road, greet him not with words nor with silence. Tell me, how will you greet him?"

Mumon's Comment

If you can answer Goso exactly, it will be extremely heartening. If you cannot answer properly yet, then you must do your best to watch out everything.

Meeting the man of the Way on the road,
Greeting him not with words, nor with silence.
Give him an uppercut;
Then he will understand you at once.

Case 37

Joshu's Oak Tree in the Garden

A monk asked Joshu, "With what intention did Bodhidharma come to China?" Joshu answered, "The oak tree in the front garden."

Mumon's Comment

If you grasp Joshu's answer precisely, there is no Shakyamuni Buddha before you and no Maitreya Buddha after you.

Words do not express fact,
Phrases do not reveal the delicate motion of mind.
He who accepts words is lost,
He who adheres to phrases is deluded.

Case 38

Goso's Buffalo

Goso asked, "A water buffalo goes out of his 'enclosure.' The head, the horns, and the four legs go through, but why doesn't the tail, too?"

Mumon's Comment

If you can open your one eye [to the question] and say an awakening word, you will be able to repay the Four Obligations and help the Three Bhava being saved. If you still have not gotten it, take a close look at the tail and awake yourself.

If the buffalo goes through, he will fall into the abyss;
If he retreats into the enclosure, he will be butchered.
This little bit of a tail,
That is a strange thing indeed!

Case 39

Ummon and the Word Trap

As soon as a monk stated, "The radiance of the Buddha quietly and restlessly illuminates the whole universe," Ummon asked him, "Are these you are reciting not the words of Chosetsu Shusai?"

The monk replied, "Yes, they are."

Ummon said, "You are trapped in words!"

Afterwards Shishin brought up the matter once more and said, "Tell me, how was the monk trapped in words?"

Mumon's Comment

If you are able to grasp Ummon's unapproachable accomplishments and follow through the monk's corruption [of being trapped in words], you will be the leader of humans and Devas. If not, you cannot even save yourself.

A fish meets the fishhook in a rapid stream;
Being too greedy for the bait, the fish wants to bite.
Once his mouth widely opens,
His life is already lost.

Case 40

Kicking the Water Jar

During his stay under Master Hyakujo, Isan was a cooking monk. As Master Hyakujo wished to send a monk to found the new monastery called the Great Mount I, Master Hyakujo told the chief monk and all other monks that he would choose the one who would demonstrate himself as the best among them.

Then Master Hyakujo brought out a drinking-water jar, put it down, and said, "You cannot call it a water jar. Then what will you call it?"

The chief monk said, "One cannot call it a wooden stick."

Then, when Master Hyakujo turned to Isan, Isan kicked the jar and walked away.

Master Hyakujo laughed and said, "The chief monk lost it to Isan."

He made Isan the founder of the Great I-san Monastery.

Mumon's Comment

Master Isan had indeed rare courage, but he could not jump out of Master Hyakujo's trap. After examination of the outcome, Isan took over the heavier burden for the easier job. Why? Look, Isan took off the cook's headband and put himself in steel cuffs [of the founder of the monastery].

Throwing away strainers and cooking spoon,

Isan kicks the jar and settles the disputes.
Unhindered by the multiple hurdles, he gives a kick with the toe.
Even Buddha becomes pieces.

Case 41

Bodhidharma's Peace of Mind

Bodhidharma sat facing the stone wall. The Second Patriarch of Chinese C'han [Zen], Suika, stood long in the thick snow. Finally, he severed his own arm and presented it to Bodhidharma. He said, "Your student cannot pacify his mind. You, the First Patriarch, please, give me peace of mind!"

The First Patriarch replied, "Bring that mind, and I will calm it down!"

The Second Patriarch said, "I search for it everywhere, but I cannot find it!"

Bodhidharma replied, "I have already pacified it for you!"

Mumon's Comment

That toothless old chap from India proudly traveled ten thousand li over the ocean [to China]. This was indeed as if he deliberately raised waves where there was no wave. At last, he got only one disciple, who was maimed by cutting off his own arm. Alas, he was a fool indeed.

> The First Patriarch from India taught straightforwardly;
> A series of all the troubles has initiated from him.
> The one who disturbed the calm world
> Is Boddhidharma, you indeed!

Case 42

A Woman Comes Out of Meditation

The wisest Bodhisattva Manjusuri, who is supposed to be next in order to Shakyamuni Buddha, found that the Buddha's gathering was adjourned and each was going back to his or her land. Observing one woman still deep in meditation near Shakyamuni, Manjusuri properly bowed and asked Shakyamuni Buddha, "That woman has been able to reach that state of Enlightenment, and why have I not?"

Shakyamuni replied, "Bring her from the Samadhi and ask her yourself!"

Manjusuri went round the woman three times and snapped his fingers, and yet she was undisturbed in meditation. So Manjusuri held her high up in his hand and brought her to the first of three meditative heavens [totally detached from any lust] and exhausted all his mystical powers in vain [to awaken her].

Observing this, Shakyamuni said, "Even a hundred thousand Manjusris could not awaken her from Samadhi. There resides Mo-myo [Avidya] Boddhisattva, the lowest of all, below this place past twelve hundred million lands. He alone can raise her from her deep meditation."

No sooner had the Shakyamuni spoken than that Boddhisattva sprang up out of the earth, bowed, and paid his homage to Shakyamuni. By Shakyamuni's order, Mo-myo Boddhisattva snapped his fingers. Instantly the woman came out of meditation and stood up.

Mumon's Comment

The old chap, Shakyamuni, is extraordinary indeed, able to produce such a village theater stage. Now then, tell me: "Why was Manjusri, the highest and wisest of the seven Boddhisattva, unable to bring her out of meditation? Why was Mo-myo Boddhisattva, the lowest of all, able to do so? Should you obtain and live this complete understanding of it, you will attain the great samadi within this mundane world of delusion and attachment."

> Whether the one who could bring her out of meditation, or the other who could not,
> Both of them obtained freedom.
> The one wore the mask of god, the other, a devil's mask in that theater;
> Even the failure is artistic indeed.

Case 43

Shuzan's Bamboo Spatula

Master Shuzan held out his bamboo spatula and asked, "If you call this a bamboo spatula, you give umbrage [to the principle of Zen]. If you call this no bamboo spatula, you violate the law [of common sense]. What will all of you call this?"

Mumon's Comment

Should you call this a bamboo spatula, you would give umbrage. Should you call this no bamboo spatula, you would betray the law. Both to speak out will not do, and no word will be of any use either. Quickly say, quickly say!"

Bringing out the bamboo spatula,
Shuzan demanded the order of life or death.
Being put to either the umbrage or the betrayal,
Even Buddha and Patriarchs would beg for their lives.

Case 44

Basho's Staff

Master Basho said to his disciples, "If you have the staff, I will give it to you. If you have no staff, I will take it away from you!"

Mumon's Comment

This staff helps you cross the river with the shattered bridge. The staff leads you back to your village in the moonless dark night. If you call it the staff, then you will go right into hell like an arrow.

Whether one is deep or shallow,
It lies in the palm of the hand which holds the staff.
The staff supports the heaven and maintains the earth;
Wherever the staff freely goes, it will propagate the true
  teaching.

Case 45

Who Is He?

To Tozan, Master Hoen the Fifth Patriarch said, "Shakyamuni and Maitreya Boddhisattva, both are His slaves. Well, tell me: Who is He?"

Mumon's Comment

Should you be able to clearly realize who he is, it would be as if you met your own father at the crossroads, as you do not have to ask your own father who he is.

Do not use another's bow and arrow.
Do not ride somebody else's horse.
Do not discuss someone else's faults.
Do not try to know some other person's business.

Case 46

Proceed Beyond the Top of the 100-Foot-High Pole

Master Sekiso said, "You are at the top of the 100-foot-high pole. How will you make a step further?"

Another Zen Master of Ancient Times said, "One who sits on top of the 100-foot pole has not quite attained true enlightenment. Make another step forward from the top of the pole and throw one's own body into the 100,000 universes."

Mumon's Comment

Should there be any who is able to step forward from the top of the 100-foot pole and hurl one's whole body into the entire universe, this person may call oneself a Buddha. Nevertheless, how can one step forward from the top of the 100-foot pole? Know thyself!

> Should one be content and settle on top of the
>   100,000-foot pole,
> One will harm the third eye,
> And will even misread the marks on the scale.
> Should one throw oneself and be able to renounce one's
>   life,
> Like one blind person leading all other blind persons,

One will be in absolute freedom [unattached from the eyes].

Case 47

Tosotsu's Three Barriers

Master Tosotsu, setting up the three barriers, always tried the pursuer of the Way: "To search for the Way, the Zen student tries to grasp one's own nature and be enlightened. Now where is your true nature?"

Secondly, "Once having grasped one's own nature, one is free from birth and death. If then, one's eyeballs have dropped dead, how can one be free from life?"

Thirdly, "Being free from birth and death, one instantly knows where to go after death. Being dead and the body dispersed into the four elements, where then does one go?"

Mumon's Comment

Whoever can pass these three barriers will be a master anywhere. Whatever happens, this person should be able to become the founder of Zen. Should one be not yet capable of answering these three questions, this person must diligently chew them well to finally comprehend them. Humble meals fill one's stomach, and chewing them well, one will never starve.

To instantly realize is to see endless time.
Endless time is this very moment.
If one sees through the thought of this very moment,
At this very moment, one can see through the one who sees through.

Case 48

The One Road of Kempo

A student monk asked Master Kempo, "I understand that all Buddha of the whole universe enter the one road into Nirvana. Where is this one road?"

Kempo raised his walking stick, drew the figure "one" and said, "Here it is."

Later, this monk went to Umon to ask the question. Umon, turning around his fan, said, "This fan will reach the thirty-third heaven and hit the nose of Sakra Devendra, the highest deity in these heavens. It is like the giant carp of the Eastern Sea tipping over with its tail a rain cloud to have the rain pour down."

Mumon's Comment

The one master walks on the deep ocean and raises dust. The other, standing on the tip of the high mountain, fills the heaven with white waves. The one holds the point, while the other liberates everything; together each supports the profound teaching with one hand. Kempo and Umon are dangerous, like two equally powerful camels colliding. No one in the world equals them. Seen from the truth, however, even Kempo and Mumon did not know where this one road really is.

They reach the goal before taking the first step.

They complete the speech before their tongue moves.
Even if they have had foresight long before,
the origin of the road lies away ahead of their foresight.

Epilogue by Mumon

    The words and the actions left by Buddha and the patriarchs in these forty-eight Koans are as precise as laws and judgements, and therein nothing superfluous is contained. They turn the student monk's brain upside down and hollow out his eyeballs. They are here in order that each one of you will immediately grasp truth and must not try to obtain it vicariously from others. Should there be anyone who thoroughly appropriates everything, the person would seize the true meaning of all Forty-eight Koans, as listening to a small portion of them. To such a person, there is no gate to enlightenment, nor steps to the search. He may go through the gate with no concern for the gatekeepers, as Gensho said, "It is the gateless that is every entrance to realization, and to be aimless is the genuine aim of the master."

    Haku-un also said, "Why can one not go through this very gate, although it is so obvious?" Such stories are indeed as meaningless as mixing milk with red clay. If you can pass these Forty-eight Koans through the Gateless Gate, you will step on me, Mumon, under your foot. If you cannot pass through the Gateless Gate, you will betray yourself. As often said, it is easy to illuminate the realization that everything is empty, but it is difficult indeed to elucidate the knowledge of distinctions. If you are able to edify the wisdom of differences, the universe will be well at peace.

BOOMER BOOKS™

Readable Type
for People in their Prime

Boomer Books are not "large-print" books; they are books that are designed for comfortable reading, with ample line spacing, hanging punctuation, and type that is justified optically and by paragraph rather than one line at a time. Boomer Books are set in Matthew Carter's Charter typeface, which follows traditional old-style book types but with three differences: narrow proportions for economical use of space; a generous letter-height to improve readability; and sturdy, open letterforms that ensure legible printing in any environment. The result is a typeface that is handsome, versatile, and above all, readable. (The Boomer Books logo illustration is by John Held Jr., artist exraordinaire of the 1920s Jazz Age.) We hope you enjoy Boomer Books! You'll find them all at www.boomer-books.biz.